Michelle Wie: She's Got the Power!

Cynthia A. Dean
AR B.L.: 3.5
Points: 0.5   MG

Michelle Wie

She's Got the Power!

by Cynthia A. Dean

Reading Consultant:
Timothy Rasinski, Ph.D.
Professor of Reading Education
Kent State University

Content Consultant:
Dr. Richard K.B. Ho, M.D., FAAP
Hawaii State Golf Association
U.S. Golf Association
Regional Affairs Committee

Red Brick™ Learning

Published by Red Brick™ Learning
7825 Telegraph Road, Bloomington, Minnesota 55438
http://www.redbricklearning.com

Library of Congress Cataloging-in-Publication Data
Dean, Cynthia A., 1970–
  Michelle Wie: she's got the power! / by Cynthia A. Dean; reading
consultant, Timothy Rasinski.
    p. cm.—(High five reading)
    Includes bibliographical references and index.
    ISBN 0-7368-5746-X (soft cover)—ISBN 0-7368-5736-2 (hard cover)
    1. Wie, Michelle—Juvenile literature. 2. Golfers—United
States—Biography—Juvenile literature. 3. Women golfers—United
States—Biography—Juvenile literature. I. Rasinski, Timothy V. II. Title.
III. Series.
GV964.W49D43 2006
796.352'092—dc22

                                     2005012347

Created by Kent Publishing Services, Inc.
Designed by Signature Design Group, Inc.
Edited by Jerry Ruff, Managing Editor, Red Brick™ Learning
Red Brick™ Learning Editorial Director: Mary Lindeen

Photo Credits:
Cover, NewsCom; page 4, Kirk Aeder/Icon SMI Photos; pages 9, 13, Donald
Miralle, Getty Images; page 11, Ronen Zilberman, EPA Photos; page 14,
Stuart Franklin, Getty Images; page 18, Neal Preston, Corbis; page 19, 30,
Associated Press, A/P; page 20, Steve Helber, Associated Press, A/P; page 22,
Douglas Healey, Associated Press, A/P; pages 24, 29, Eric Alcantra, Associated
Press, A/P; page 27, Chris Trotman, Corbis; page 33, Dave Bowman, The
Daily Press/Associated Press, A/P; pages 35, 38, Brian Myrick, Daytona Beach
News-Journal/Associated Press, A/P; page 36, Paul J. Smith, Icon SMI Photos;
A/P; page 41, Baughn Youtz, Zuma Press

Printed in the United States of America.

1 2 3 4 5 6 11 10 09 08 07 06 05

Table of Contents

Michelle Wie studies a putt at the Sony Open in Hawaii.

CHAPTER 1

Taking on the Big Boys

Michelle Wie (WEE) stands over her golf ball.
*A large crowd watches. She has to make this **putt**.*
*Michelle is playing in her very first **PGA** event.*
It is the Sony Open in Hawaii. She is 14 years old.

Just a Kid

Michelle Wie had a big year in 2004.
That year, Michelle became the youngest
golfer ever to play on the PGA Tour.
At the Sony, she wasn't just the youngest.
She was the only female against 143 men.
Michelle also was an **amateur**.

---

putt (PUHT): a soft swing to make a golf ball go in the hole
PGA: short for *Professional Golfers' Association of America*
amateur (AM-uh-tur): someone who plays a sport for fun, not money

Playing Against Men

Many people thought Michelle didn't belong at a men's event. Often, men are stronger than women. Men usually hit the ball farther. The men's courses are longer than the women's.

Michelle didn't agree. She knew she was strong. She could hit a **drive** 310 yards (283 meters). She knew she could keep up with men. In fact, she thought she could beat them. "I don't feel **intimidated**. I hit as long as [men] and sometimes I hit farther," Michelle said.

Would Michelle keep up at the Sony Open in Hawaii? She would soon find out.

---

drive (DRIVE): a hard golf swing to make a golf ball go a long way
intimidated (in-TIM-uh-date-ud): frightened by others

Michelle Wie can hit the ball more than 300 yards (274 meters). That is longer than three football fields end to end!

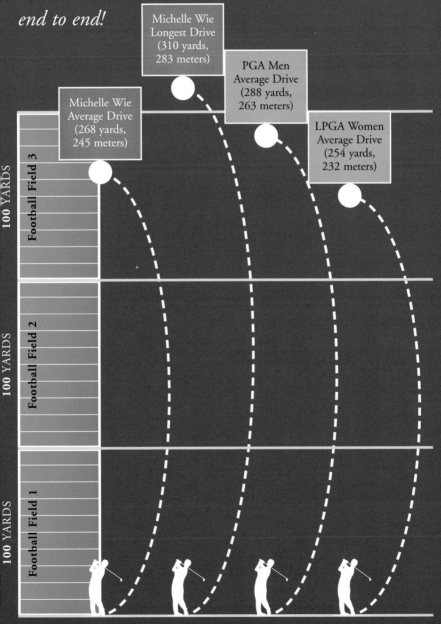

Michelle Wie
Longest Drive
(310 yards,
283 meters)

PGA Men
Average Drive
(288 yards,
263 meters)

Michelle Wie
Average Drive
(268 yards,
245 meters)

LPGA Women
Average Drive
(254 yards,
232 meters)

100 YARDS — Football Field 3

100 YARDS — Football Field 2

100 YARDS — Football Field 1

First PGA Event

At the 2004 Sony Open in Hawaii, no one knew what to expect from Michelle. Many men had never played a PGA match against a woman. Many said that Michelle would fail.

During the match, Michelle kept calm. Her drives sailed high into the air. Her putts rolled smoothly into the holes. Everyone was surprised. Soon it was clear that this girl could keep up with the guys.

Michelle missed the **cut** by just one **stroke**. Still, she beat 48 men. She also made history. Michelle shot the lowest score by a female in a men's event. Not bad for a 14-year-old!

---

cut (KUHT): the halfway point of a golf contest; those who make the cut may play the final two rounds
stroke (STROHK): one swing of a golf club that is added to a player's score

Ernie Els with Michelle during the
Sony Open in Hawaii

Only a few amateur golfers are invited to play on the PGA Tour. To play with the pros, you have to be a great amateur golfer!

High Hopes for 2005

Michelle returned to the Sony Open in 2005. She hoped to do even better. People asked, "How far will she go this year?"

Michelle was **ambitious**. She liked to win. She wanted to do things other women hadn't. "I'm not interested in making the cut," Michelle said. "I'm interested in finishing in the top 20."

Making the top 20 is hard. Michelle would need to beat more than 120 men to do it! "That would be really cool," Michelle said.

---

ambitious (am-BISH-uhss): having a strong wish to succeed

Michelle watches the ball after one of her big drives.

Off Course

In the 2005 Sony Open in Hawaii, Michelle struggled. The wind blew hard. It blew her ball off course. Each hole she got further behind. She missed the cut.

"My putts didn't go in. I took too many shots. It did not go the way I had hoped for. At least I'm not in last place," Michelle said.

Michelle was not used to failure. But she learned to accept it and move on.

Broken Dreams?

Michelle had dreamed big. She had dreamed of being the first woman in 60 years to make the cut at a PGA event. Her dream didn't come true. But she never gave up. Where did Michelle get such **grit**?

---

grit (GRIT): the strength to keep going even though it is hard

Michelle misses a putt at the 2005 Sony Open in Hawaii.

*Michelle's mother, Bo, is a former
Korean women's amateur champion.*

— Chapter **2** —

Growing Up

At age 4, Michelle took her first golf swing.
She wasn't much taller than the golf club.
But even then, she could strike the ball hard.
Like that ball, Michelle would go far!

Backyard Lessons

Michelle's parents taught her to play golf. They gave her lessons in the backyard of their home in Hawaii.

Michelle's parents are Korean. Her father is Dr. B.J. Wie. Her mother's name is Bo. Both B.J. and Bo play golf very well. In fact, Bo was once Korea's women's amateur champion.

A Young Learner

Michelle didn't just play golf at a young age. At 1 year old, she learned the alphabet. By 2, she could read. At 3, she began to sign her name!

Michelle is proud that she learns quickly. "My first memory is going down by the pool and reading a sign that said, 'Warning: Don't Dive.' I could read it and knew it had something to do with danger," said Michelle.

Just a Bit Wild

When Michelle was 5, she could hit the ball 100 yards (91 meters). "Michelle has always liked to hit the ball hard," said B.J. "Sometimes it would go right, sometimes left, but it didn't matter. She just wanted to hit it hard."

Her **slices** scared her neighbors, though. What if she broke a window? What if she hit someone? It was time to move out of the backyard!

Around this time, Michelle began to copy one of her golfing **idols**. He held the golf club in a special way. Can you guess who it was?

---

slice (SLISSE): a golf shot that goes way off to the right for a right-handed golfer and to the left for a left-handed golfer
idol (EYE-duhl): someone people love and admire

Michelle on the golf course with her parents

At the Golf Course by Age 7

B.J. and Bo first took Michelle to the golf course when she was 7. Michelle learned more about golf. She copied how Tiger Woods gripped the club. Michelle locks the little finger of her bottom hand with the index finger of her top hand. This grip hooks the hands together. Then they won't slip. The grip worked well. Michelle hit the ball straighter.

The interlocking grip

No Slowing Down

At the golf course, some golfers groaned when they saw little Michelle ahead of them. They thought she might slow them down. But they soon found out Michelle shot better than they did.

Beating Dad and Mom

Michelle and her parents played golf together for many years. "When Michelle was 7, we could beat her," said B.J. "When she was 8, she started beating us." By the time Michelle was 9, her parents stopped trying to beat her.

Michelle's parents, B.J. and Bo Wie, watch Michelle play.

Juggling School and Golf

A day for Michelle is much like a day for any student her age. She goes to Punahou *(POOH-nah-hoh)* School in Hawaii. School is important to Michelle. She hopes to go to college.

But her life is different from other kids' lives, too. After school, Michelle plays golf. Then she goes home to work out. She eats dinner and finishes her homework. Michelle also leaves time to watch TV or listen to music.

Michelle is also a great sleeper. She once slept for 16 hours straight!

*Michelle hits off the tee during the U.S. Girls'
Junior Championship.*

Not Yet Ready

Michelle was taller and stronger than many players her age. By age 10, she could drive the ball more than 220 yards (201 meters). But she couldn't control her shots. She hit balls into the water. Some went into the trees. She also took too many putts to finish a hole. Sometimes she struggled to play well.

Michelle played her first **junior** event before she turned 10. She later played in more amateur events. She hit the ball with plenty of power. Now, could she control her power and learn to win?

---

junior (JOO-nyur): for younger players

*Michelle at age 11 could hit
the ball farther than most adults.*

CHAPTER 3

The Young Champ

"I just want to push myself to the limit," Michelle said. *"I want to be known as [someone] that changed the world and changed how people think."*

Not Like Other Girls

Michelle wasn't like many 11-year-old girls. She was 5 feet 9 inches tall. She could hit the ball 270 yards (247 meters). With a breeze, the ball might go 300 yards (274 meters). Many adults could not hit the ball that far.

Tough Training

Michelle had lots of talent. But she also **trained** very hard. Michelle's coach, Casey Nakama (NAH-kah-mah), helped her control her drives. On weeknights, Michelle practiced for 4 hours. On weekends, she practiced for 7 to 8 hours.

In the summer, Michelle started practice at 9:30 a.m. She played 18 holes of golf. Then she practiced her swings and putts until it was dark.

Would Michelle's size, strength, and skill help her beat professional women? Should she stick to playing against juniors? At age 11, what would you do?

---

train (TRANE): to practice a skill so that you get better

Golf's New Face

In May 2001, Michelle played in Hawaii's top women's amateur event. It was the Jennie K. Wilson Invitational.

Michelle was 11 years old and playing in an adult event. Was Michelle **nervous**? Could she control her shots?

Michelle would prove that she could compete.

---

nervous (NUR-vuhss): fearful or worried

Youngest Champ Ever!

As the Jennie K. began, Michelle played well. Her drives went 40 to 50 yards (37 to 46 meters) farther than anyone else's. She was the leader after the first round.

But Michelle's strong play and good luck didn't last. She seemed to lose her **touch**. The ball just wouldn't go where she wanted.

Still, Michelle stayed calm. She **focused** on her game. She knew what to do to win. It worked. Michelle won by nine shots!

Michelle made history just by playing in the Jennie K. It was the first time players under 16 could play in the event. Now, 11-year-old Michelle was the new Jennie K. champion!

---

touch (TUHCH): a special quality or skill
focus (FOH-kuhss): to concentrate very hard

The Big Wiesy

Soon, some great golfers began to notice Michelle's big swing. Her swing even earned her a nickname: "The Big Wiesy." What do you think that meant?

> "The reporters kept asking me how young I was. They [didn't believe], I guess, that I'm only 11," Michelle said.

Michelle said some of her sixth-grade classmates called her a "golfing geek."

"When you see her swing—when you see her hit
a golf ball—there's nothing that prepares you for it.
It's just the scariest thing you've ever seen," said
PGA pro Fred Couples.

— Chapter 4 —

The Big Wiesy

Michelle's swing takes "girlpower" to a new level.
She hits the ball as far as most men. Some people
say she has the best women's golf swing in the world.
Will it take her where she dreams of going?

Michelle Gets Noticed

Michelle's big golf swing got noticed.
Golfers couldn't believe that a young girl
could hit the ball that well.

One PGA golfer, Tom Lehman,
compared Michelle to the great Ernie Els.
Els' big swing makes golf look easy.
So Els is nicknamed, "The Big Easy."
Lehman called Michelle, "The Big Wiesy."

What's in a Name?

The nickname added to Michelle's fame. It also added to people's hopes for Michelle. This was a lot of **pressure** for someone so young. Could Michelle handle it?

Away from Home

In 2003, Michelle played in her first **national championship**. It was the 2003 Women's Amateur Public **Links** Championship in Palm Coast, Florida. Could she win away from home? Could she win her first national title?

---

pressure (PRESH-ur): a burden or strain
national championship (NASH-uh-nuhl CHAM-pee-uhn-ship): a contest in which people from all over a country play
links (LINGKSS): another name for a golf course

Michelle hits out of the long grass along the 16th fairway during the U.S. Women's Amateur Public Links Championship.

Stuck in the Sand

At the start of the tournament, Michelle took the lead. Then, she hit the ball into a sand **bunker**. It is hard to hit a ball out of the sand. Often, a player is happy just to land the ball anywhere safely.

Michelle studied the shot. Which club should she use? She picked one. Her dad didn't agree with Michelle's club choice. But Michelle knew which club she wanted. "I'm going for it," Michelle said.

She swung. Crack! The ball flew out of the sand and over a water **hazard**. It landed right on the **putting green**! From there, Michelle took control of the match.

---

bunker (BUHNGK-ur): a large hole on a golf course usually filled with sand

hazard (HA-zurd): an area on a golf course that is difficult to hit a shot from, such as a lake, stream, pond, or bunker

putting green (PUHT-ing GREEN): an area with low-cut grass where players putt the ball

A National Title

Michelle won the match by one stroke. She also became the youngest champion in **USGA** history. It was her first national title. "It's pretty cool," Michelle said. "I'm happy out of my mind."

Michelle holds the championship cup after winning the 2003 USGA Women's Amateur Public Links Championship.

USGA: short for *United States Golf Association*

What Is an Amateur Golfer?

Amateur golfers play golf for fun. They don't get money if they win.

Amateur golfers play in both local and national tournaments. They are also invited to play in professional tournaments. But only a few spots go to amateur golfers. To play with the pros, you have to be an outstanding amateur golfer!

Michelle hits a drive at the Bay Mills Open in Brimley, Michigan.

Playing with the Women

By December 2003, Michelle was one of
the top amateur players in the United States.
She was third on the 2003 *Golf Digest* list
of top 10 amateur women's golfers. But
Michelle was three or more years younger
than the others.

She Has What It Takes

Michelle proved she could golf with the best.
But where would her big swing take her?

"Yeah, I'd love to [win] the Masters," said Michelle.

CHAPTER 5

The Future

At the moment, Michelle lives a double life.
She is a high school student and a rising golf star.
What are Michelle's plans for the future?

The Masters

In 2005, Michelle was invited to play in several **LPGA** events. Michelle also hopes to be invited to some PGA events. Her biggest hope is to win an LPGA and a PGA title.

One day, Michelle also wants to play in the **Masters** Tournament. The Masters is one of golf's biggest events. Women have never played in the Masters before.

LPGA: short for *Ladies Professional Golf Association*
Masters (MASS-turz): one of the four PGA major golfing events

School Matters

Michelle cares about more than just golf. School comes first for Michelle. She is a very good student. She studies Japanese, physics, English, art, history, and math. Her favorite subject is math.

Michelle plays golf after school. She competes in tournaments during the summer and spring breaks. That way, she doesn't miss much school. Michelle believes students should stay in school and wait until they are 18 to become professionals.

After high school, Michelle plans on going to college. Stanford University in California is her first choice right now.

Giving Back

In 2005, Michelle joined the Miracle **Birdie** Club. Fans could **donate** money for each birdie Michelle made at the Sony Open in Hawaii. The donations helped sick children in Hawaii.

Michelle Wie is a winner. She shows that with hard work and **determination**, dreams can come true.

What do you think will happen to Michelle? Will she ever win a PGA title? One thing is certain: Michelle has the grit to make it in the golfing world.

---

birdie (BUR-dee): a score on a hole one stroke less than par
donate (DOH-nate): to give
determination (di-TUR-min-AY-shuhn): a firm decision to do something

Epilogue

Michelle Wie Time Line

1989 — Born to parents B.J. and Bo in
Honolulu. Her middle name is Sung.

1996 — At age 7, plays her first 18-hole round.

2000 — At age 10, is the youngest player
to play in a USGA Women's
Amateur Public Links Championship.

2001 — At age 11, wins the Hawaii State
Women's Stroke Play Championship.
Wie is the event's youngest winner.

2001 — Wins the Jennie K. Wilson
Invitational. She is the youngest winner.

2002 — At age 12, is the youngest player
ever to play in an LPGA Tournament.

2002 — Wins the Women's Division of
the Hawaii State Open by 13 strokes.

2003 — Plays in her first LPGA major tournament. It is the Kraft Nabisco Championship. She finishes 9th. Wie is the youngest player to make an LPGA cut.

2003 — At age 13, wins the U.S. Women's Amateur Public Links Championship. Wie is the youngest-ever winner of the event.

2004 — At age 14, plays in her first PGA Tour event. It is the Sony Open in Hawaii. She misses the cut by one stroke.

2004 — Finishes 4th in the first LPGA major contest of the year.

2005 — At age 15, plays in the PGA Sony Open in Hawaii. She misses the cut by seven strokes.

Glossary

amateur (AM-uh-tur): someone who plays a sport for fun, not money

ambitious (am-BISH-uhss): having a strong wish to succeed

birdie (BUR-dee): a score on a hole one stroke less than par

bunker (BUHNGK-ur): a large hole on a golf course usually filled with sand

cut (KUHT): the halfway point of a golf contest; those who make the cut may play the final two rounds

determination (di-TUR-min-AY-shuhn): a firm decision to do something

donate (DOH-nate): to give

drive (DRIVE): a hard golf swing to make a golf ball go a long way

focus (FOH-kuhss): to concentrate very hard

grit (GRIT): the strength to keep going even though it is hard

hazard (HA-zurd): an area on a golf course that is difficult to hit a shot from, such as a lake, stream, pond, or bunker

idol (EYE-duhl): someone people love and admire

intimidated (in-TIM-uh-date-ud): frightened by others

junior (JOO-nyur): for younger players

links (LINGKSS): another name for a golf course

LPGA: short for *Ladies Professional Golf Association*

Masters (MASS-turz): one of the four PGA major golfing events

national championship (NASH-uh-nuhl CHAM-pee-uhn-ship): a contest in which people from all over a country play

nervous (NUR-vuhss): fearful or worried

PGA: short for *Professional Golfers' Association of America*

pressure (PRESH-ur): a burden or strain

putt (PUHT): a soft swing to make a golf ball go in the hole

putting green (PUHT-ing GREEN): an area with low-cut grass where players putt the ball

slice (SLISSE): a golf shot that goes way off to the right for a right-handed golfer and to the left for a left-handed golfer

stroke (STROHK): one swing of a golf club that is added to a player's score

touch (TUHCH): a special quality or skill

train (TRANE): to practice a skill so that you get better

USGA: short for *United States Golf Association*

Bibliography

Baldridge, Dean, Donald Emerick, Jim Fisher, and Ken Kebow. *Tiger's Tips: Beginner's Golf for Kids.* Coal Valley, Ill.: Quality Sports Publications, 1998.

Gordon, John. *The Kids Book of Golf.* Tonawanda, New York: Kids Can Press, 2001.

Greene, Susan. *Consider It Golf: Golf Etiquette and Safety Tips for Children!* Chelsea, Mich.: Excel Publishing, 2000.

Murray, Drew and Jeremy Sterling. *Caddywhack: A Kid's-Eye View of Golf.* Ann Arbor, Mich.: Clock Tower Press, 2003.

Ruthenberg, Stephen. *Golf Fore Kids.* Lansing, Mich.: RGS Publishing, 1997.

Useful Addresses

Ladies Professional Golf Association
100 International Golf Drive
Daytona Beach, FL 32124

**The Professional Golfers' Association
of America**
100 Avenue of the Champions
Palm Beach Gardens, FL 33410

Internet Sites

Ladies Professional Golf Association
http://www.lpga.com

**The Professional Golfers' Association
of America**
http://www.pga.com

Index